HOW-TO LIBRARY

BUILDING BIRDHOUSES

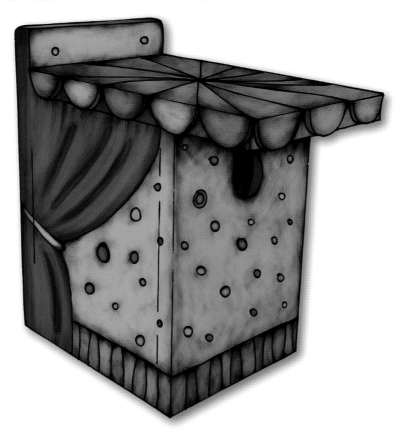

By Dana Meachen Rau • Illustrated by Kathleen Petelinsek

CHERRY LAKE PUBLISHING • ANN ARBOR, MICHIGAN

CHERRY
LAKE
Publishing

A NOTE TO ADULTS:
Please review the instructions for these craft projects before your children make them. Be sure to help them with any crafts you do not think they can safely conduct on their own.

A NOTE TO KIDS:
Be sure to ask an adult for help with these craft activities when you need it. Always put your safety first!

Published in the United States of America by Cherry Lake Publishing
Ann Arbor, Michigan
www.cherrylakepublishing.com

Content Adviser: Dr. Julia L. Hovanec, Professor of Art Education, Kutztown University, Kutztown, Pennsylvania

Photo Credits: Page 4, ©Kletr/Shutterstock, Inc.; page 5, ©old apple/ Shutterstock, Inc.; page 6, ©David B. Petersen/Shutterstock, Inc.; page 8, ©jannoon028/Shutterstock, Inc.; page 12, ©Tyler Olson/Shutterstock, Inc.; page 32, ©Tania McNaboe

Library of Congress Cataloging-in-Publication Data
Rau, Dana Meachen, 1971–
  Building birdhouses / by Dana Meachen Rau.
    p. cm. — (Crafts) (How-to library)
  Includes bibliographical references and index.
  ISBN 978-1-61080-478-3 (lib. bdg.) — ISBN 978-1-61080-565-0
(e-book) — ISBN 978-1-61080-652-7 (pbk.)
1. Birdhouses—Design and construction. I. Title.
  QL676.5.R38 2013
  728'.927—dc23   2012014013

Cherry Lake Publishing would like to acknowledge the work of The Partnership for 21st Century Skills. Please visit *www.21stcenturyskills*.org for more information.

Printed in the United States of America
Corporate Graphics Inc.
July 2012
CLFA11

The author would like to thank Dan Porga for sharing his woodworking tips and expertise.

HOW-TO
LIBRARY

TABLE OF CONTENTS

For the Birds

Some birds like to build their nests inside hollow tree holes.

Birdhouses make attractive decorations in a backyard. But the best birdhouses aren't just nice to look at. They are good for birds, too!

Most birds build nests out of twigs, grass, bark, and other natural materials. Some like cozy **enclosed** spaces inside the trunk of dead trees. Others prefer to nest in the fork of a tree, above a light fixture, or even in the letters of a big store sign.

If you want birds to move into your backyard, you can build an inviting home for them. This book shows you how to make a basic nesting box for birds that like enclosed spaces. It also shows you how to build a platform for birds that prefer nesting in the open air.

Research the birds that live in your area. Then build a birdhouse to attract them. Watch to see who moves in!

WHAT'S GOING ON IN THERE?

Birds usually start nesting in spring. They lay a **clutch** of eggs. Most often, the female bird sits on the eggs to keep them warm as the babies grow inside them.

The babies hatch out of the eggs when they are ready. Some types of birds are born with their eyes closed. They have no feathers. Their mother brings them food. Others are born with soft fluffy feathers. They peck on the ground to find food. As baby birds grow, they try to fly. They leave the nest when they are ready to live on their own.

Mother birds bring food back to the nest for their hungry babies.

Home Sweet Home

You need to build a birdhouse a certain way to make the best home for birds.

The Right Size

Different **species** of birds prefer different birdhouse sizes. You have to consider the size of the floor, the height of the walls, and the width of the entrance hole.

Some bird species will only build their nests in homes that are a certain size or shape.

The Right Location

Find a spot that gets some sun—but not during the hottest part of the day. The box should face away from the wind. Don't hang it in a busy place where a lot of people pass by. Place it in an area with a nearby branch where a mother bird can **perch**.

The Right Material

Wood stands up well to all kinds of weather. It also **insulates** well. There are two types of wood: hardwood and softwood. Softwood is usually easier for sawing and drilling. Cedar and white pine are good softwoods to use for birdhouses. Materials such as metal or plastic can be harmful to birds. A birdhouse made from a metal coffee can or license plate can heat up too much in the sun. A plastic milk jug does not provide enough insulation from cool temperatures outside.

SOME COMMON BIRDHOUSE NESTERS
Here are some birds that might use the birdhouses in this book.

Enclosed Houses:
House wrens
Chickadees
Nuthatches
Titmice

Platform Nesters:
American robins
Phoebes

Books, bird-watching Web sites, and many other sources have specific house dimensions and more complete lists if you have other birds you want to attract to your area. Check them out!

A Safe Shelter

A well-built birdhouse will last for many years.

Your home is built to be a strong and safe shelter for you. Birds need the same type of house.

Keeping It Dry

The roof should hang over the front of the birdhouse to keep rain from getting into the entrance hole. The front, back, and sides should surround the floor and extend a little beyond it so rain can't leak in. Make sure all of the pieces are fitted snugly against each other.

Drill small holes in the floor so water has a place to drain out. Drill **ventilation** holes along the top of each side so fresh air can get into the small space.

Keeping It Clean

Build your birdhouse with a side that can open. This will allow you to look in on the nest. Open the house when the baby birds have all left. Clean out the old nest so the next bird to move in can build a fresh one.

Clean out the birdhouse in the fall before winter sets in. Then it will be ready for new birds in the spring.

Keeping It Safe

House cats, raccoons, opossums, and other animals may try to get to the eggs and baby birds. An overhanging roof will make it harder for **predators** to reach in from above. Make sure the latch of your hinged side is closed tight. Some builders wrap the tree trunk with a sheet of metal so animals can't climb past it and get to the birdhouse.

House sparrows and European starlings compete with **native** birds for nesting boxes. House sparrows and starlings need holes 1½ inches (3.8 centimeters) in diameter or larger. If possible, make your holes smaller to keep them out. Perches also attract sparrows and starlings. You don't need one on your birdhouse. Your birds can get in without one.

Basic Materials

To build a birdhouse, you need wood, a way to cut it into pieces, and a way to hold the pieces together.

- *Wood*—You'll see all types of boards if you visit a lumber store. A 1 x 6 is a board that is 1 inch (2.5 cm) thick and 6 inches (15 cm) wide. But it's actually a little smaller. The wood was measured before it was dried. Look for a board that is straight and not **warped**. Avoid boards with lots of **knots** or splits.

  You don't need much wood for a birdhouse. If you know a woodworker or builder, ask if he or she has scraps you can use.

Use these tools to do the following jobs:
- *C-clamps*—to hold a board to the workbench and keep it from moving as you saw, hammer, or drill it
- *Handsaws*—to cut wood. A crosscut saw is used to make cuts across the **grain**. A ripsaw cuts with the grain.
- *Drills and bits*—to make holes in wood. You can attach different size bits, depending on how big you need the hole to be.
- *Claw hammer*—to pound in and remove nails

- *Nails*—to hold pieces of wood together. **Galvanized** nails are best for outdoor use.
- *Screws and screwdrivers*—to hold pieces of wood together. A Phillips head screwdriver turns cross-slot screws. A straight screwdriver turns straight-slot screws.
- *Awl*—to make small holes for starting nails and screws
- *Hinge*—to allow a door to swing open
- *Waterproof wood glue*—to glue on wooden decorations
- *Steel tape measure*—to measure long pieces of wood
- *Ruler*—to make smaller measurements
- *Square*—to make sure your angles are straight
- *Pencil*—to mark your measurements on wood
- *Sandpaper*—to smooth out the rough edges and surfaces of wood
- *Exterior paint and brushes*—to decorate your birdhouse

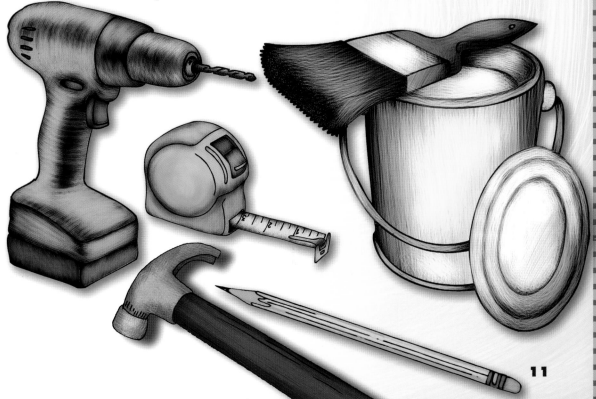

Basic Birdhouse Building

Precise measurements are important to any woodworking project.

Keeping safe should be your number-one concern. *Always have an adult help you with these projects.*

You can keep yourself safe in other ways, too. Wear safety glasses when you are working to keep bits of wood from getting in your eyes. Wear a dust mask when sanding so you don't inhale sawdust.

Wear sturdy, closed-toe shoes to protect your feet in case you drop a hammer or a piece of wood. Sawdust can be slippery, so keep your workspace clean. Wear work gloves to protect your hands.

Your Workbench

You may have a table to use. If not, you can make one by placing a piece of plywood over two sawhorses, crates, or old chairs. Use clamps to hold the plywood in place.

How to Measure

Hook the steel tape measure to the end of a board and pull it out to the length you need. Use a pencil to mark the measurement on the wood. Hold one edge of the square on the side of the board. Line up the other edge with your measurement and mark it with a pencil line. Extend the line to the edges of the board. Always double-check your measurements. If you cut a piece of wood even a little bit too short or too long, it can mess up your entire project!

How to Saw

Clamp the board to your workbench. The width of the saw's blade and teeth is called the kerf. Place the saw on the wood so that the kerf is on the side of your line that will not be used for the birdhouse. Pull the saw back toward you slowly. Do this a few times to make a small groove. Then continue sawing back and forth in longer strokes along the line. Do not try to force the saw through the wood. Simply let the saw blade cut at a steady pace. Support the end of the wood as you complete the cut so that it doesn't fall to the floor.

How to Drill

Clamp the wood to your bench so the part you want to drill is hanging off the end. Or clamp it on top of a piece of scrap wood on the workbench. Hold the drill straight up and down as you drill the hole.

How to Fasten Boards with Nails

Hold the nail in position with your fingers. Gently tap on the head of the nail so it starts to pierce the wood. Once it feels secure, remove your fingers and hit the nail with a little more force to drive it into the board.

Keep the nail as straight as possible. If it starts to bend or slant, remove it with the claw end of the hammer.

How to Fasten Boards with Screws

You need a pilot hole to start a screw. Drill a small hole with a bit that is smaller than your screw. You can also poke a hole in the wood with an awl. Place the tip of the screw in the hole and turn the top with a screwdriver.

How to Sand

Rub sandpaper along the wood in the same direction as the grain on the surface and edges of the wood.

How to Paint

Many birdhouses look nice without paint. But painting can be a great way to make your birdhouse unique. If you want to add color, try using **muted** shades that look more natural.

Exterior paint that cleans up with water works well for outdoor use. Never paint the inside of a birdhouse. The paint could be **toxic** to birds.

How to Hang

Wrens are one of the only birds that don't mind their houses freely hanging from a tree. Attach eye hooks to the top of the box. Then hang it from a sturdy wire or cord. You could also hammer a sturdy nail into a tree or the side of a building and hook the birdhouse onto it. If you don't have a tree to hang your birdhouse from, you can mount it on the top of a post.

Only certain birds will nest inside freely hanging houses.

Wren House

In summer, house wrens can be found all over the United States. These small songbirds like backyards and parks with trees, grass, and bushes. A female wren lays about 3 to 10 eggs at a time.

If you want chickadees to be able to use this box, too, make the hole $1\frac{1}{8}$ inches (2.9 cm). This hole will still keep out starlings and house sparrows.

Materials

1 x 6* white pine board cut to the following dimensions (*see pages 12–14 for measuring and cutting tips*):

*A 1 x 6 board actually measures ¾ x 5½ inches.

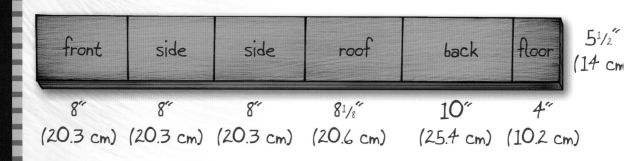

front	side	side	roof	back	floor	5½" (14 cm
8" (20.3 cm)	8" (20.3 cm)	8" (20.3 cm)	8⅛" (20.6 cm)	10" (25.4 cm)	4" (10.2 cm)	

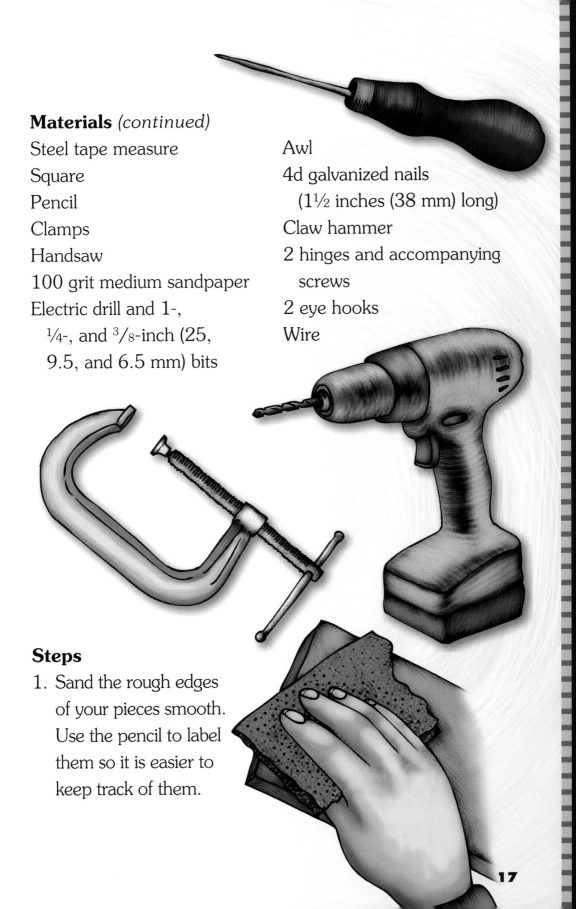

Materials *(continued)*

Steel tape measure
Square
Pencil
Clamps
Handsaw
100 grit medium sandpaper
Electric drill and 1-,
    ¼-, and $^3/_8$-inch (25,
    9.5, and 6.5 mm) bits

Awl
4d galvanized nails
    (1½ inches (38 mm) long)
Claw hammer
2 hinges and accompanying
    screws
2 eye hooks
Wire

Steps

1. Sand the rough edges
of your pieces smooth.
Use the pencil to label
them so it is easier to
keep track of them.

Cut all of your pieces before you start putting them together.

2. Drill the following holes (*See pages 12–13 for drilling tips*):

   Front: One 1-inch (25-mm) hole, 1 inch (2.5 cm) from the top for the entrance

   Both sides: Three ¼-inch (6.5-mm) holes, 1 inch (2.5 cm) from the top and the sides

   Back: One or two ⅜-inch (9.5 mm) holes, 1 inch (2.5 cm) from the top for hanging

   Floor: Four ⅜-inch (9.5-mm) holes, 1 inch (2.5 cm) from all sides for drainage

3. Hold the floor piece against a left side piece ¼-inch (0.6 cm) up from the bottom. Trace the edges along the side piece. This will give you guidelines for nailing. Use the awl to mark the side piece with three pilot holes evenly spaced within your guide.

4. Start the nails by hammering them into the pilot holes until they just start to poke out the other side. Clamp or hold the side piece steady and hold the floor piece in position. Continue hammering the nails to attach the two pieces together.

5. Next, attach the back piece to the side and floor. Trace a

guideline on the back piece, mark your holes, and start the nails. Hold the back and side against each other. Continue nailing to attach them.

6. Attach the front to the side and floorpieces as described above.

7. The right side will open like a door. Place the right side piece in position. Place the hinges along one side. Mark the screw holes. Make pilot holes with the awl. Screw the hinge screws to hold the hinges in place.

8. On the opposite side of the door, attach one eye hook to the door and one to the front edge. Keep the door closed with a small twist of wire.

9. Next, attach the roof. Mark a guideline along the back piece and start the nails. Then hold the roof in place and nail it in. Add nails along the front and left sides. Don't nail the right side or you won't be able to open your door.

Attach your hinges so they swing outward.

KEEP THEM STRAIGHT! If your nails aren't straight, they might poke into the inside of the box. This could be dangerous for your birds.

Big Top Birdhouse

Bring the circus to your own backyard by painting a birdhouse to look like a big top tent. Use a variety of colors, but don't make them too bright. Softer, natural colors are best for a birdhouse. You can mix muted colors by combining a little gray paint with the color of your choice.

Birdhouse designs can be fun and festive decorations in your yard.

Materials

Wren house
  (*see directions on
  pages 16–19*)
150 grit fine sandpaper
7 small wooden craft circles
Small saw
Waterproof wood glue
Pencil
Ruler
Exterior paint in muted colors
Paintbrushes

Steps

1. Sand all the sides of the box to make a smooth surface for painting.

2. Ask an adult to cut the wooden circles in half with a small saw. Sand the edges smooth. Glue them all around the roof edge. Be sure they do not overhang your door.

3. Draw your design onto your box. Maybe include a striped border along the bottom and curtains on the sides. Measure to find the center of the roof. Draw lines from this center point to the edges of the half circles.

4. Paint the roof and half circles in **alternating** colors. Paint the curtains, border, and the rest of the box in any color combination you want. Let it dry.

5. Add more painted color details, such as polka dots or other designs to match your circus theme. Let the paint dry.

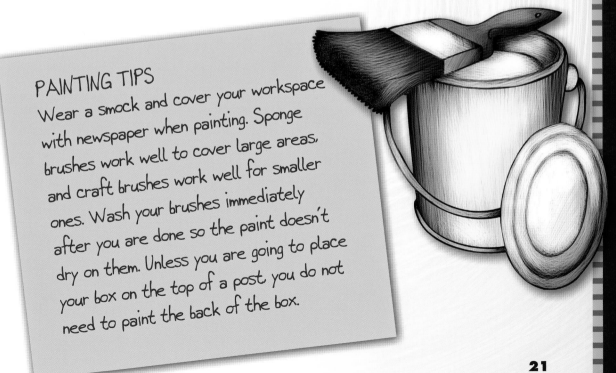

PAINTING TIPS

Wear a smock and cover your workspace with newspaper when painting. Sponge brushes work well to cover large areas, and craft brushes work well for smaller ones. Wash your brushes immediately after you are done so the paint doesn't dry on them. Unless you are going to place your box on the top of a post you do not need to paint the back of the box.

Camouflage Cabin

Camouflage is something that blends into the surroundings. Make a birdhouse that blends right into the tree it's hanging on by covering it with natural materials.

Materials

Wren house (*see directions on pages 16–19*)
Fallen bark and twigs
Pinecones
Pruning shears
¾-inch (19 mm) finishing nails
Hammer
Waterproof wood glue

Start with an undecorated wren house.

Steps

1. Collect bits of fallen bark and twigs from the trees in your yard, wooded space, or woodpile.
2. Use pruning shears to trim some of the pieces of bark and twigs to the size of your birdhouse.
3. Place the pieces onto the sides of your house and attach them with the hammer and nails. Cover the top, sides, and front, but make sure you can still open the door. Also be sure to leave the ventilation holes and entrance hole uncovered.
4. Trim smaller pieces to fill in the gaps and small spaces. Glue on pinecone decorations.

Make sure each piece of bark is attached securely.

Robin Platform

Robins are large common songbirds that often bring news of the coming spring. They feed on insects, fruit, and worms. The female builds a nest with grass, twigs, and mud on branches with leaves for shelter. They do not like to build their nests in enclosed spaces. Phoebe birds also prefer platforms for nesting.

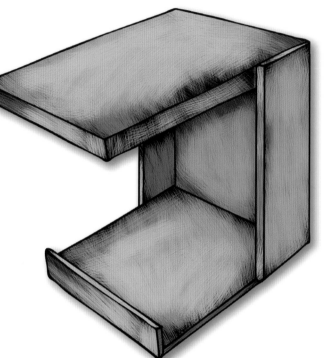

Materials

1 x 8* white pine board cut to the following dimensions (*see pages 12–14 for measuring and cutting tips*):

A 1 x 8 board actually measures ¾ x 7¼ inches.

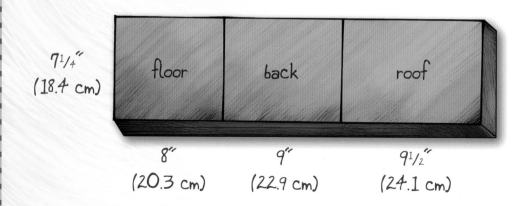

7¼" (18.4 cm)

floor — 8" (20.3 cm)

back — 9" (22.9 cm)

roof — 9½" (24.1 cm)

Materials *(continued)*

Two ¼ x 3-inch (0.6 x 7.6 cm) pine boards cut 9¾ inches (24.8 cm) long for the sides

One ¼ x 1½-inch (0.6 x 3.8 cm) pine board cut 7¼ inches (18.4 cm) long for the front

Steel tape measure

Square

Pencil

Clamps

Handsaw

100 grit medium sandpaper

Awl

4d galvanized nails (1½ inches (38 mm) long)

Claw hammer

Steps

1. Sand the rough edges of your pieces smooth. Use the pencil to label them so it is easier to keep track of them.

2. Hold the floor piece against the back piece. Trace along the bottom edge of the board to draw a guideline for nailing. Use the awl to mark the back piece with three pilot holes evenly spaced along your guide.

3. Start the nails by hammering them into the pilot holes until they just start to poke out the other side. Then clamp or hold the back piece steady and hold the floor piece in position. Continue hammering the nails to attach the two pieces together.

4. Next, attach the roof piece to the back piece in the same way.
5. Attach the side boards, nailing them into the top, back, and floor.
6. Attach the front board to the floor edge.

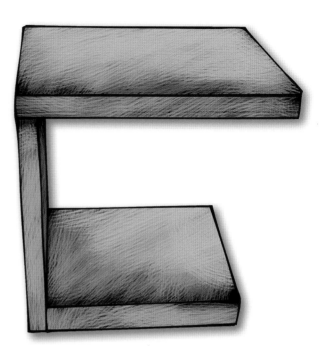

Use the longer piece as a roof.

You can decorate a basic platform with many themes. Your birdhouse will be even more fun if it is decorated with your own design! Remember to use muted colors and don't paint the inside. Paint the bottom so the platform looks nice from below when you look up at it.

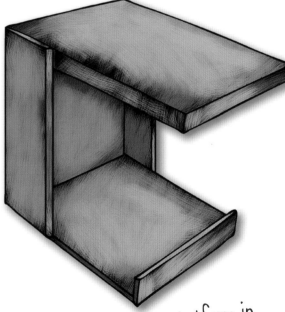

Paint your platform in your favorite colors.

Sky Box

Clouds are just one of the many patterns you might use to decorate your platform.

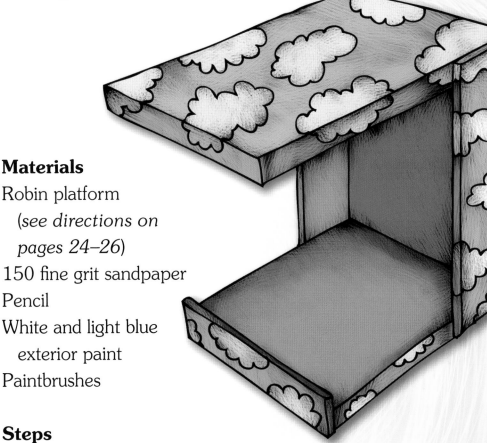

Materials

Robin platform
  (*see directions on
  pages 24–26*)
150 fine grit sandpaper
Pencil
White and light blue
  exterior paint
Paintbrushes

Steps

1. Sand all the sides of the platform to make a smooth surface
   for painting.
2. Draw cloud shapes all over the top, sides, bottom, and
   front of the box.
3. Paint the space between the cloud shapes light blue. Let
   the paint dry.
4. Fill in the cloud shapes with white paint.

Up on the Farm

Birds are sure to build nests in this barn!

Materials

Robin platform
  (*see directions on
  pages 24–26*)
150 fine grit sandpaper
Gray, red, and white
  exterior paint
Paintbrushes
Wooden craft sticks
Pruning shears
Waterproof wood glue

Steps

1. Sand all the sides of the platform
   to make a smooth surface for painting.
2. Paint the roof of the platform gray. Paint the sides, bottom,
   and front of the platform red.
3. When all the paint is dry, sand the painted surfaces to give
   your birdhouse a weathered barn look.
4. Cut the craft sticks in half with pruning shears. Sand the
   ends smooth. Paint them with white paint and let them dry.
5. Use wood glue to attach the sticks to the front of the box
   like a fence. Paint white fence details between the sticks.
6. Paint barn doors and windows on the sides.

Bird-Watching

Now that you have become a birdhouse builder, become a bird-watcher. Spy on birds from a window or a quiet place in the yard where you won't scare them away. Use binoculars to identify birds and watch their habits. Hopefully they'll discover your birdhouse and settle in.

You can also build your birds a source of food and water. Provide them food by planting bushes and shrubs that grow berries, or by setting up a bird feeder with seed. Give them water for drinking and bathing by adding a birdbath to your outdoor space.

Make your yard inviting to birds. They may decide to call it home!

NESTING MATERIALS

You can help birds find soft materials to weave into their nests. Leave these treats outside for birds to find:

- Dryer lint
- Bits of string and yarn
- Hair from your hairbrush
- Dog hair or cat hair
- Small scraps of cloth
- Dental floss

Try placing some of these items inside a mesh bag like the ones that onions come in at the grocery store. Hang the bag from a tree. Birds will love these helpful items!

Glossary

alternating (AWL-tur-nay-ting) going back and forth between two things

clutch (KLUHCH) a group of eggs laid at the same time

enclosed (en-KLOZED) surrounded on all sides

galvanized (GAL-vuh-nized) coated with steel, iron, or zinc to prevent rusting

grain (GRAYN) the lines on the surface of a piece of wood

insulates (IN-suh-layts) holds in heat

knots (NAHTS) round, hard spots on wood where branches once grew

muted (MYOO-tid) soft, not bright

native (NAY-tiv) found naturally in a certain area

perch (PURCH) to stand or sit on the edge of something

predators (PRED-uh-turz) animals that hunt other animals for food

species (SPEE-sheez) a group of living things that can mate with each other to produce offspring

toxic (TAHK-sik) poisonous or harmful

ventilation (ven-tuh-LAY-shuhn) the movement of fresh air into a space and stale air out of a space

warped (WORPED) twisted, curved, or bent out of shape

For More Information

Books

Kelsey, John. *Woodworking.* East Petersburg, PA: Fox Chapel Publishing, 2008.

Schwarz, Renée. *Birdhouses.* Toronto: Kids Can Press, 2005.

Thompson, Bill. *The Young Birder's Guide to Birds of North America.* Boston: Houghton Mifflin Harcourt, 2012.

Web Sites

Audubon: Just for Kids

http://web4.audubon.org/educate/kids/

Play fun games and learn about different bird species.

Bird Feeders Direct: Bird Houses

www.birdfeedersdirect.com/bird-houses/

Learn more about different kinds of birdhouses.

BirdWatching Bliss: Bird House Dimensions

www.birdwatching-bliss.com/bird-house-dimensions.html

Find out which birdhouse sizes will attract different types of birds.

Index

About the Author

Dana Meachen Rau is the author of more than 300 books for children on many topics, including science, history, cooking, and crafts. She creates, experiments, researches, and writes from her home office in Burlington, Connecticut.